Table of Contents

Dedication

This book's intended audience is for those people that are precontemplating, contemplating, or have taken action to have *Less Debt, Less Stress*. This book may not be as useful for seasoned wealth builders. Through personal stories, and factual knowledge, I will guide you through the basics of building credit, budgeting and saving.

I am also dedicating this book to those of us that did not grow up with a proper introduction to money management. Some of us did not have finances discussed as a dinner table conversation. That is okay. Forgive your family and yourself for your financial stress.

According to the ACLU (2020), Baltimore, City Public Schools Reported that 45% of students do not have computers and/or internet access for remote learning. This book is dedicated to

these beautiful children that do not have a fare
path to education.

Prelude

I never imagined that I would ever write a book. Literature is not exactly my true love. My mom was a Language Arts teacher growing up! She is the sole reason I was able to average a B in English. Even in my college years, I could still count on her to compose an intro paragraph to kick off what would be an A paper.

So here I am embarking on this journey on my own. I got this…

Growing up I knew the ins and outs of my mother's wallet. I knew her payroll schedule, how much she earned, what bills were due, and of course what was remaining to spend. We indeed spent it… ALL OF IT. We would shop, see a movie and order takeout all in one weekend. Did I mention that this was all on one source of income? Unfortunately, by the following weekend we were back waiting for pay day. My mom always had a budget. Sticking to it, was is a whole other story.

Buying things fills voids and it is what kept us busy. Those very things also kept us in a constant game of cat and mouse. We were chasing pay day with a new game plan to save. We are staying in all weekend! We are raiding the pantry and cooking what we have. We have a new budget to stick to! There is nothing else we need to buy! I am not sure who were convincing, but none of these lines prevented us from spending every dime! Well, all except what was needed to make it another two weeks.

I do caution you that money is not a direct link to happiness. I had an amazing childhood. I was encouraged to be creative, to be caring, to be strong, and to love hard. We were, however, very bounded. Movimiento es vida!

"By age 3, your kids can grasp basic money concepts. By age 7, many of their money habits are already set". Procrastinating, over shopping, overeating – I am guilty of all the above. The daily work exists to shape new ways of thinking. Reshaping our outlook to the unhealthy ways of processing life is tough work and it is never ending. I was able to define healthy habits by introducing new ideas and experiences into my daily regimen.

Less Debt, Less Stress will provide you with the tools, tips, and the reality checks needed to live a life of financial freedom. We will explore getting out of debt, building a great credit score, and creating an actual savings. We will work through these topics by exploring our barriers to change. How we respond to pain, how we manage our stress, and how we view change are all important factors to building long-term wealth.

With an open mind, this will be our reminder that we do not need a new job to spark change. The work starts now! A close friend once told me that "It's not about how much you make; it's about how you spend it" and I whole heartedly believe this to be true. I could never be at peace with knowing that I have a wealth of unshared information. Let us sip tea shall we!

The Pledge

Change often requires us to be uncomfortable. I know I was uncomfortable when I sacrificed my entire lifestyle for 4 years to become a CPA. Looking back, it was well worth it, but those times were also strenuous. My faith, my support system, and my sound commitment to building generational wealth is what pulled me through. What I would change about those times, is how I processed stress, and how I managed my relationships.

To get the most of this literature, I want you to read the following aloud. Twice! The first time that you read this pledge, it should be for you to _gain an understanding of what is being asked of you._ Reading the pledge for the second time should be for you to _accept what is being asked of you_.

"The past is the past! I will be honest about my true financial status. I will keep an open mind. I will be intentional about my goals for improvement. I will find a friend to hold me accountable. I will communicate my intent to do better with my accountability partner. I am committed to doing whatever it takes to achieve happiness. I will not shy away from the truth as my truth is the tour guide of my life."

FUEL

A **FORCE** needed to **UNDERGO** the process of creating new **ENERGY** in our everyday **LIFESTYLES**

Fight or flight! This is the normal reaction to the idea of changing unhealthy behavior. We can choose to let our troubles metastasize, or to let them metabolize.

I cannot believe that I am telling you this, but I tend to lose toenails. Yes, like whole toenails! Every so often, the nail of one of my toes will detach from the nail bed and a new nail grows underneath. It is more disgusting than it is painful, trust me.

I love to run! A playlist containing a mix of R&B, Afro-Beat and Rap pushes each stride. Beat by beat, I sweat out my worries and I give thanks to the dawn of a new day. I know the thought of running 13.1 miles can make some people cringe but, it turns me on. As peaceful as the race is, the recovery is not always as pretty. Aches, bruises, tense muscles and for me broken toenails. When this first started happening, I would ignore it. Yes, I would let the toenail begin to lift from my skin and I would not clip it off. Water would accumulate underneath, and fungus would begin to grow. Now not only was I down to 9 toenails but I also had fungus. In the summertime I had no patience to give to fungus, so why not slap some nail polish on top and keep it pushing. At this point, I had 9 toenails, fungus, and discomfort from the chemicals in the nail polish. Trifling AT. IT'S. BEST. Finally, enough was enough and I began researching a solution. Can you believe it? The combination of mouthwash and vinegar is a common at-home remedy to kill fungus. Since the fungus grew over time, it did take some time to nurse and rocking cute sandals was no longer a short-term option for me.

Why didn't I just cut the dead nail and allow a new one to grow?! I instead allowed the pain to metastasize through reckless procrastination. I was so afraid of what it would look like to not have a nail. What would people say when I am wearing open toe sandals! How long will it take for the new nail to grow? This fear kept me in denial and pushed me two steps backwards.

So, there I was finally fungus free and without a toenail. I will be the first to tell you it was not half bad and little people noticed. I purchased new running shoes in a larger size, and I was back to hitting the pavement to my favorite tunes. Although I waited far too long, when I did allow change to metabolize, it provided me the fuel I needed to create new habits for a healthier lifestyle.

In the late 1970's researchers James Proschaska and Carlo DiClememnte were researching ways to help people quit smoking. They were curious as to why some smokers were able to quit on their own, while some required further treatment. The results were that people quit smoking only when they were ready. Through this research, they established the Transtheoretical Model (TTM), also known as The Theory of Change. TTM found that change is intentional and thus, this theory focuses on the decision making of the individual undergoing change.

Basically, if we are going to change it will not just happen! "I will get around to it." Ummm no you will not!

It is this feeling that comes over us when we have had enough. We have all felt it in relationships with friends, lovers and family right! We set measurable deadlines for these feelings of change. Girl the next time she does it I will have to say something! If he does not get it together in 6 months I am out! We must keep that same energy with the self- sabotage we are doing when it comes to personal finance. A third of our lives are spent working! We earn money to pay bills and experience life. Experiences are great but at what point do we sacrifice the short-term experiences and tangible things for long-term legacy. We must be the force to create change in our everyday lives.

As we move through each phase of the TTM I will tell you what each step looks like in our everyday lives, what pushed me to take my desire for change to the next level, and what advice I have for crushing financial goals with ease!

The Transtheoretical Model

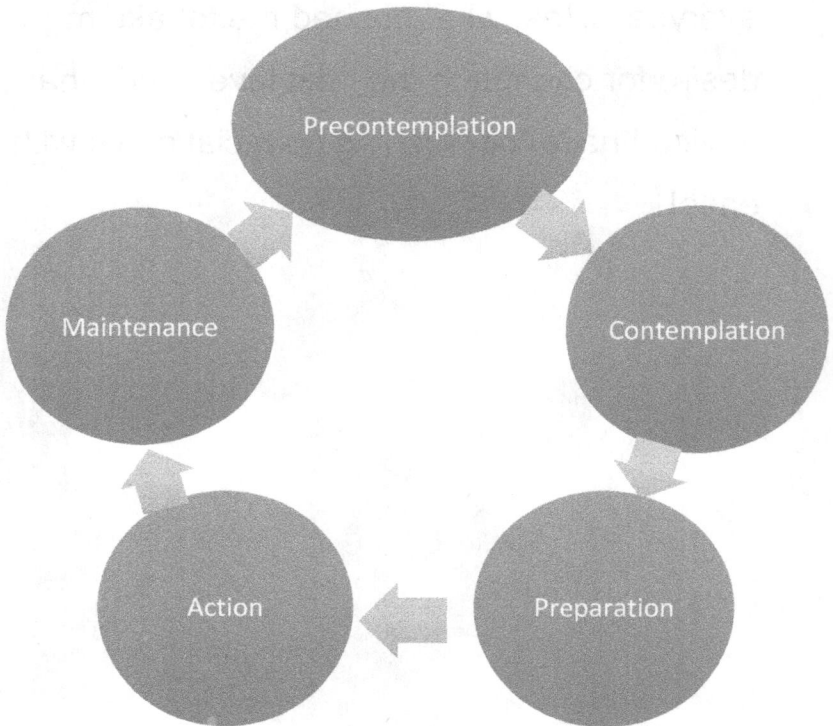

This chart depicts the phases of the Transtheoretical Model. It is also known as the Stages of Change Model. We move through this cycle as we act on those nasty habits preventing us from gaining real progress. This chart will guide our behavior as we build long term wealth.

SOLID

STUCK ON LIVING IN DENIAL

The purpose of Solid, this chapter of the book, is to understand our stress and thoughts as we consider the idea of change. **The idea of restructuring who we are can be daunting. After all, we have lived with these habits for years and this causes us to be STUCK ON LIVING IN DENIAL**

Precontemplation

When I graduated with my undergraduate degree in 2008, I had accumulated $43,000 in student loans. This is not bad in terms of college debt. Currently, tuition and fees average about $26,290 per year for a four-year public university and $35,830 for a private college. I managed to save cost by staying in-state and applying for numerous grants and scholarships. Thank you so much College Bound! They were instrumental in securing tuition grants that were a huge help to my family and me.

I was grateful for this small amount of debt, but I had deep regret for the $10,000 of credit card debt I racked up at Frostburg State University (FSU). Although I was in state, I moved 2 and a half hours away from Baltimore to Frostburg, Maryland. The cost of food now that I was on my own, clothes as I experimented with my style, fun adventures, trips back home etc. it all added up.

That was just at FSU though. I ended up transferring my senior year and I graduated a year and a half later with my degree in accounting from Morgan State University (MSU). Go bears! During this time at Morgan I added an additional $5K to my credit card debt. This time, what was my excuse? I was back in Baltimore living with my mom, so groceries and other miscellaneous living cost were covered. I was taking 18 credits in the evening, but I worked during the day. I had a job as a bookkeeper at a restaurant and I worked a 40-hour weekly schedule as a tax auditor during my final semester at MSU.

You are what you ingest! My image truly used to consume me. I was addicted to constantly ordering new clothes, false eyelashes, makeup, hair extensions and the list goes on. I had to have the look! It is nothing wrong with treating yourself and accessorizing your image with enhancements. However, I could not afford the lifestyle that I was absolutely enamored with. During this time in life, my boyfriend was beginning to purchase a home. The information that he received from the lender began to circulate within our conversations. This was literally the first time in life that I gave thought to credit. I had a good state job, a car that I owned, so I assumed I was doing well for that time in life. Well when I checked my credit score, I was sadly mistaken.

Credit cards pray on college students. 1 in 5 students' graduate college with over $5,000 in credit card debt and 1 out of 10 students graduate with over $10,000 in credit card debt. I was the latter. I mean as cruel as it is, the scheme makes sense. Attracting a younger demographic means a longer term to pay off interest arrangements. They also know that moms and dads who are super proud of us will provide bail in the blink of an eye! In most cases, credit card companies pay the universities to market on college campuses. On top of that, they also receive kickbacks for students that sign up. At the time, there were practically no policies around lending to minors. All you had to do was fill out an application and you were approved! There was no job verification, or credit check. Crazy right! Currently, there is greater legislation in place that sets policy around lending to minors under the age of 18. If you do not have job income, you must have a co-signer on your application for credit! Although times have changed, there is still a lack of clarity around the job income requirement. We all know that work study or any college campus job for that matter is just pocket change.

I was stuck on living in denial. I never even told my family that I took out credit cards. I always have been the type to want to handle things on my own. Even if made matters worse! Pride cometh before the fall. My weakness is truly asking for help. I knew my mother was doing her best to manage the household and the last thing I wanted to do was add additional stress to her plate. I did not realize that If I had spoken to my family about this, I would have found out that I was not alone in my credit card debt! I would have also discovered that it was not just my family.

According to the Transtheoretical Model, being SOLID means, you are in the phase of Precontemplation. During this phase, we are not even aware that our behavior is problematic. We have no intention of changing for the foreseeable future, which is defined as 6 months. We are more focused on the cons of a shift in behavior and the idea of altering our way of thinking seems quite burdensome.

Now, I will dive into what this looks like for us in layman's terms. I warn you that these examples can be quite triggering. If you are SOLID you WILL find yourself relating to at least one of these instances of precontemplation. Do not the close this book or figure this is a good time to do something different with your day. No! Please push through. I beg of you. Precontemplation is one of the hardest phases to move through because 99% of the work is mental. If you stop now you will be stuck on living in denial.

Pay day loans are literally the devil in a dress! These loans send the wrong message. They are saying that it is okay to live above our means. Why change our behavior when we can just borrow a little something to hold us over right? There is this myth that the average borrower of pay day loans is low income and living in poverty. That could not be more untrue. The average borrower is a homeowner with annual income of $47,620.

About 70% of the borrowers of payday loans are using them for their regular recurring expenses, such as rent, utilities, etc. An even scarier, but relatable fact is that about 12% of the U.S. population has a poor or bad credit score that would leave us with alternative lending such as payday loans as one of the few options available when we are in a bind.

There are a few reasons we should stay far away from these financial traps. First, the loan must be paid off by pay day! This is absurd compared to personal loans that give you one to two years to pay off principal plus interest. I also believe that the cost of borrowing these loans to be unfair! The finance charge ranges from $15 to $30 to borrow $100. For two-week loans, the interest rates range from 390 to 780% APR. Most borrowers are unable to pay off the loan by pay day because our regular bills have not changed and neither has our behavior.

So, what happens? We roll over the loan until next pay. With the high interest rates, we never have the money to pay off the full balance. This leaves millions of Americans unable to ever pay off these loans!

Our history with on time bill payments are another clear indicator if we are SOLID. Our ability to pay our bills on time is bigger than keeping the lights on. This is one of the biggest factors in maintaining a good credit score. In fact, it accounts for 35% of our FICO score. If we have otherwise spotless credit, a ding in payment history can knock our credit score down at least 100 points. If we already have bad credit, it does damage but not to as large of a degree!

It is important that we stay aware of what bills affect our credit and it gets tricky! Most leasing companies do not report our timely rent payments to the credit bureau. However, if we get evicted than it will most likely appear on our credit report! We should not be afraid to ask leasing companies to report to the credit bureau on our behalf! After all, this is the largest monthly expense and every point counts. Although leasing companies may not report to the credit bureau, applying for a new apartment often requires a reference from our prior landlord. There is little room to escape paying our rent on time. This goes for other household bills such as utilities. These companies often skip out on reporting positive changes, but they with report accounts that need to be collected on. Unfair I know!

There is a lengthy list of reasons why we do not pay our bills on time. This causes us to do some prioritizing. We may not have enough income to pay our household bills, celebrate a friends b-day, pay for childcare, and treat ourselves to the bi-weekly manicure and pedicure we truly need and deserve!

So, what do we do? Most of us think in terms of necessity. This is usually our rent, car insurance, internet, cell phone bill, childcare, and groceries. Everything else is secondary! Utility companies are usually the most patient with disrupting our services, so they are last on the list to be paid. When it comes to rent or mortgage, we usually give the landlord half of a payment and attempt to pay the rest throughout the month. This conceptually makes sense, but there are negative consequences, A low credit score, mental stress, overeating, staying in unhealthy relationships because they benefit us financially, and the list goes on! According to business wire, half of Americans are paying a bill late each month. The inability to make on time bill payments is a clear sign that we are living beyond our means. Oh, and news flash! If we have not changed this behavior yet, we are stuck on living in denial!

Do you owe money to the IRS? There is a large chance that you do! Millions of Americans are just not paying their taxes. According to the latest IRS data, roughly 14 million taxpayers owe $131 billion in taxes and penalties to the federal government. These numbers have climbed in recent years, showing signs that Americans are facing increasing hardships. We are not alone in this. Corporations who collect payroll taxes from employees are required to submit the employee and employer tax to the IRS. Many are underreporting taxable wages and they are getting away with it! They are doing it for the same reasons we are! We simply do not have the money! Yeah, it feels a bit different when you hear that companies are doing it. At the end of the day, these are our hard-earned earnings that they are just holding on to! However, the reasoning behind it is just the same. Or it could be corporate greed, but that is a topic for a different book!

So, at this point, it should be clear to you that you are in financial distress. To many of us, the work to change the cycle seems as massive as the Great Wall of China - so we figure why change. We are getting by just, fine right?

Post college, the only way that I was able to make it through this precontemplation phase was to share my frustrations with someone. That person for me was my boyfriend! Sharing this journey with a close friend or family member is not optional! Who else will hold us accountable? Clearly, we cannot do this for ourselves or we would be reading a different book. Be wise about choosing the accountability partner. I am a firm believer that we should only ask for advice from people who can help us in that subject area. For example, do not ask a friend that lacks consistent relationship history for relationship advice. Do not bring your best friend along for car shopping if she is driving a G-wagon that she cannot afford. We should keep this same mindset when choosing our financial accountability partner.

At the time, my boyfriend was literally the only person I knew in my life that had good credit and that was demonstrating progressive financial behavior. It was tough for me to confide in him because I knew that he would not let me forget that I was in debt. Affectionally called, "Coach Kendall", I knew that he would hold me to my word, and I knew that he would check me at any sign of regression.

It is also important to find someone we cannot "ghost". Not one of my more attractive traits, but I will ghost people for various reasons and sleep quite cozy at night! I am a strong believer that people come in my life for a season, reason or lifetime. The older I get, the less patience I have for making friendships work. If it does not work out there is a reason, and I love them from a distance. I am in no way promoting this behavior because I also believe that healthy communication is a much better option than going "ghost."

When finding our accountability partner make sure it is that friend that will literally beat the door down looking for us! Make sure it is someone that we have no shame in being honest with.

In the precontemplation phase, we are weighing the pros and cons of altering our unhealthy habits. However, it is so easy to retreat. So, I say with certainty and urgency to identify who this person is. It is impossible to make this 360 without a person in our life that knows our struggles and knows the plans for change.

Contemplation

We must crawl before we walk! I truly wish someone would have told me this. I had my accountability partner, and I had convinced him that I was truly ready for change. My boyfriend took note of my enthusiasm and my newfound commitment to building a good credit score. I was taking steps to research, making plans, digging into my credit report and creating the o so necessary visions boards. To reward my "good behavior", and to give into my constant nagging, he allowed me to be added as an authorized user to his Nordstrom Credit Card.

This was a great idea! An authorized user is a secondary user on a credit card. This is a huge upgrade for those who are unable to be approved for their own credit card due to having either no credit history or bad credit history. The primary card holder has the option of granting this additional user with their own physical card. The secondary user benefits from the accounts age, the positive payment history, and the amount of available credit. It is important that we only add an authorized user that we can trust. Ultimately, the responsibility of making the monthly payments still falls on the primary card holder. There should be a separate payment arrangement made between the primary and secondary user to reimburse funds that were charged throughout the month.

I was extremely grateful for his trust and his care to help me achieve financial stability. In 2 out of every 5 couples, a partner admits to lying to their spouse about financial troubles. According to a survey done by SunTrust Bank, 35 percent of all respondents that experience relationship stress said money was the primary cause of friction. Inevitably, this leads to failed relationships and divorce. The results vary by generation, but TD Ameritrade released data (2018) showing 41% of divorced Gen Xers and 29% of Boomers say they ended their marriage due to disagreements about money.

I applauded our ability to address financial issues at the age of 21. However, we were not really asking the right questions. At no point did we explore the psychology behind why my spending habits were what they were. There is a reason or logic behind every decision that we make. Even if it is subconsciously. See my unhealthy spending habits were a learned behavior from childhood. We were never without shelter, food, electricity, and a cute outfit. I learned to normalize living check to check. There was little to no shame in paying bills late for short term experiences and material things.

I was also wrong to continue blaming my youth for my poor choices. At some point in life we must be able to stand in our truth. It was easier to blame others for not helping me to explore my feelings, or past experiences than to be honest about why I was hurting. Daddy issues, insecurity with my image, boredom and the list goes on. I was not shopping because I truly needed these things, I was shopping because I was this young broken girl looking for a quick fix. Searching for love in the mall, the nail salon, and in restaurants became my vice.

My boyfriend and I did not connect these dots at the time. Our focus remained on my new positive outlook and our desire to be on the same page financially. We knew that I was making great money coming out of college and that on the surface there was no obvious issue that would prevent me from gaining financial stability.

We had it all wrong! As life threw me hurdles, my coping mechanisms remained the same. Only now, I felt the need to lie about it. I could not bear telling my boyfriend that I went to the mall and spent an absurd amount in Nordstrom. I had already felt like a burden and I did not want to add to the load. Instead, I just made sure to have the money by the time the bill was due. No harm no foul right? Not exactly, because life always has a way of catching up with us. Once my boyfriend reached his second year of grad school, he had to reduce his work hours and hold a full-time internship. This new life event caused a shift in responsibilities. Even in grad school he always managed to pay the mortgage. While I was appreciative of this, I picked up other household and daily living expenses. With this increase in bills, I was unable to camouflage the excessive spending at Nordstrom with timely bill payments. On top of that, he needed to swipe here and there for a new work wardrobe. What started out as a token of love, quickly became a point of friction in our relationship!

This became the tipping point for me! I knew that I could no longer just think about debt freedom. It was time to make that a reality. According to the TTM, the Contemplation stage occurs when we intend to start a healthy behavior in the foreseeable 6 months. During this time, we are making our pro and con list. We are debating if we have what it really takes to do this! It is normal to feel both the excitement to change and the reluctance to commit. Any small push in either direction can make all the difference.

Often, we think we are ready to face an obstacle, but in truth we have not done the work it takes to overcome said obstacle. Without this work, we find ourselves constantly in an uphill battle. We muster up just enough energy to make it up the hill, but our lack of preparation sends us back down with a feeling of defeat

Obstacles are just limitations that prevent us from obtaining our goals and achieving true happiness. The happiness and the goal both being defined by you! Have you ever wanted to go for a job but talked yourself out of it? Or tell someone special how you feel about them but opted out instead? These are examples of some everyday obstacles we face. There is no rule book to overcoming them successfully but there are a few lessons I have taken from my financial obstacles.

Being honest with myself has been the key factor to reducing financial stress associated with becoming debt free. Self-honesty is a trait that is immensely important to our growth. Without this truth, it becomes impossible for us to heal. Without this healing, we continue to use the same unhealthy behaviors to cope. We are our truth. We can hide the world from our truth, but we cannot hide the world from us. For this reason, we form this new being that we present to the world. The stress of living a double life is exhausting and limiting! It is important that we can stand in who we are.

According to Good Therapy, self-honestly leads to a sense of fearlessness. Once we become comfortable with who we are, it makes it easier to accept our weaknesses and flaws. Having this knowledge tells us what we are capable of as well as our limitations. Being honest with ourselves will only allow us to be honest with others. Along the way will be questioned about our commitment to building long term wealth. This feedback will come from those who have and have not accomplished a fifth of our goals. Regardless of their opinion on our journey, we must stay planted in the truth. This truth will be key to building healthy relationships with people that support us. Relationships can thrive when both individuals are the best versions of themselves.

Change is not something that always came easy for me and that was mainly due to burying my emotions. I had to face my demons and have some tough conversations.

Defining the Life You Want to Live

1. What matters most to me?

2 What are my goals?

3 What part's of my past am I holding on to?

4. What am I afraid of?

5. What am I willing to sacrifie?

To successfully graduate from the contemplation phase in the TTM cycle, we must define the life we want to live. Being clear about our goals helps us to prioritize our daily lives. We want each decision to be made with purpose and intent.

What matters most to you? This is the first question requiring self-honesty that I would like us to explore. It is important that we are clear of our priorities and objectives. Media, friends and the environment can pull our attention in multiple directions. We can become so consumed with what we see others doing and what we think we should be doing as a result. What we want in life becomes so grey.

During this exercise, we must be mindful of how each objective coincides with others. As an example, our key life objectives are to climb the corporate ladder, to eat healthy, and to homeschool our children. We may want to consider the time involved with securing and maintaining that VP of sales position. We should delve into how we can "have it all"? To have it all will we need a nanny? Are we okay with the idea of someone else helping to raise our children? If not, then perhaps we may need to shift our goals to be realistic to what matters most to us. Perhaps being second in command to the VP of sales will give us the time to homeschool our beautiful babies and maintain a healthy lifestyle. Genuinely think of the peaks in like when you are the happiest.

What are your goals? This is the second question requiring self-honestly that I would like us to explore. We just discovered the major things that matter to us. In a sense this is what our lives would be like in a perfect world. Our goals should be the realistic means to achieving this utopia. Goals are the game plan to achieve both happiness and long-term wealth. Be specific as possible. This makes our goals appear more achievable. Sarah Knight has written several books on prioritizing our lives to achieve a desired outcome. One of the game-changing tools I learned from her literature, is the power of defining mini-goals. This tactic right here has been critical to maintaining fuel in the monotony of self-discipline. Through our progression of the TTM cycle, there will be days and months that we are bored with life. Throwing our disposable income into debt and saving is not always fun. In our down time we are going to be researching and planning ways to invest our savings. It is easy to be fed up with this routine so setting mini goals is ultra-important. When we pay off our first credit card it is okay to treat ourselves to brunch with the girls. Be sure to set a budget and take only the cash we have available to spend!

What parts of your past are you holding on to? This the third question requiring self-honesty that I would like to explore. I can be a bit of a grudge holder. In my life, I have spent so much time being mad at people. Going on and on about what could have been, I get caught in this web of thoughts. The details are where I excel. It is important for me that I rewind all parts of the story. Instead of focusing on how we can move forward, I have been guilty of dwelling on the past. It was so unfair of me to hold people accountable for actions they have apologized for. Let it go! I am saying this with a sense of urgency. Being unable to forgive keeps us SOLID.

To build wealth we must be willing to let go of the past. We have been conditioned, especially culturally, to believe that we should organize our life in a certain pattern. We eventually inherit this pattern and become resentful that we are not living a life of truth. We can be so stuck on living the life that we defined at 21, 25 or 30! We have gotten older and we should develop goals in line with where we are currently. Some of us have been blessed to have had success in our college field of study. There are others that have found success in making career changes and taking nontraditional routes. Either way, we should find peace with letting go of who we thought we would be.

I want you to write down financial advice that you have been given. This advice could have been received intentionally or unintentionally. It is normal to manage our finances in a similar fashion of our parents. The opposite could be true as well. Perhaps we learned what not to do by observing our parents.

I want us to also explore the assets we see associated with wealth. Start with writing down the assets we currently have. This is our car, our home, designer items, cash and other liquid assets. Next to each item, indicate if it helps us to maintain or adds value to what matters most. This list will guide our truth about what parts of our past we still hold on to.

Prioritizing ourselves can be so scary! We get so used to letting life call the shots that we stop being the CEO of our own lives. So many of us look at our current experiences as permanent. We are so afraid of trying, so defeated by failure and so distant to risk. We tell ourselves all types of lies. "Why fix what isn't broken" and "You can't teach an old dog new tricks." We literally talk ourselves out of change before even trying.

What are you afraid of? This is the fourth question requiring self-honesty. We must be fearless in our journey to build wealth. Trial and error are how we learn. For me, I am afraid of not having the means to live a life of financial freedom. Not being able to provide makes me feel incapable. The only person that I am afraid of disappointing is me. Knowing this, I make goals that provide for multiple streams of income. I have become a bit of a workaholic. I must be working on some way to monetize my creative passions. Instead of running from my fears, I keep them front and center.

Sometimes our fear involves disappointing others. We must accept judgement for what it is. Doing different things likely involves criticism. According to the Tiny Buddha blog, "when someone criticizes or judges your choices, they are only showing their own misunderstanding. It is an insecure person who judges another person's choices." I am a firm believer that people can only make us feel insecure regarding things we are already insecure about. However, it is easier to blame others for the hurt. We should explore the fear bounding us to our current circumstances and aim to be the fearless version of ourselves.

What are you willing to sacrifice? This is the last question requiring self-honesty that I would like us to explore. Each person's sacrifice will be different. However, all of us must sacrifice in order to experience living the life we want to live. We must do the work to figure out what our tolerance level is for sacrifice.

For me I sacrificed friendships! This is hard for me to share with you, but I know that someone needs to hear this. I am 29 years old and I have been in a relationship with my boyfriend for a little over 10 years. For this relationship to flourish it required a huge commitment to communication, trust and consistency. Those happen to be the same ingredients needed to make any relationship prosper. Over the years I have found myself failing miserably at maintaining friendships. I am very secretive about my love life and I have no shame in that! You should not tell everyone your business and that includes family. This has caused a problem for me with friends because it is a topic that I limit my voice too. I may come off as being secretive and I understand my friends (or x friends) feeling that way about me. However, I value the up's and downs of my relationship too much to always share.

I also have put too much pressure on my friends. In my mind I needed them to be my travel partners, my confidant in low times and my cheerleader for change. This may sound reasonable. However, I learned over the years that each person in my corner may only be one of these things. It is okay to have friends that are there for a good road trip, but they may not be the best cheerleader for change. This is how I have learned to maintain friendships in recent years. I had to sacrifice my own wants to have a "best friend". Instead, I had to come to terms with having a "best brunch partner" or a "best road trip friend." I have let go of the past failed friendships. They did not work for a reason. I love them no less, but I have chosen to move on for my own healing. Now this is your time to figure out what you are willing to sacrifice to live the life you want to live.

LIQUID

LIBERALLY IN QUEST to UNVEIL our INTENTIONS for personal DEVELOPMENT

The purpose of Liquid, this chapter of the book, is expressed as a phrase that we can always refer to. In the planning and action phases of the TTM, we are **LIBERALLY IN QUEST** to **UNVEIL** our **INTENTIONS** for personal **DEVELOPMENT.** In this space we have already established a sense of freedom. Although we are just beginning to plan and act on our goals, we are no longer surrounded by hesitation and unsureness. The work has begun, and we are able to move freely without the heaviness of self-doubt. In this phase we are in quest to uncover the intentional plan we have for our life!

Preparation

If we have not been inspired to build wealth in the past, the COVID 19 pandemic should be a huge wakeup call! This unprecedented time has shown us the need for wealth building. It has forced us to rethink our overall strategy on life. Career paths, personal relationships, business strategies, living situations and the list goes on!

I know that for me, it revealed family, friendship and job dynamics that I did not know even existed! As heavy as these times are, I am truly thankful for the slower pace. It has forced me to focus on what is in front of me and not the next best thing! Not the next best idea, but the business I currently have! Not a different man but the one that has been right here all along. See that is a common issue that several us have. We are waiting for that one life change to adjust our hustle. Be that a promotion, a pay raise, getting our business started… you get the point! I like to say that financial change starts now, not pay day, but this very moment.

We do not need all these new things to live a life of financial freedom. We just need to appreciate what we have, be honest about where we are, plan to change our current circumstances, and stick to it!

This planning phase of the trans theoretical model is the 30 days leading up to the change in behavior. At this point we are fully aware of why we want to become debt free and build long term wealth. We have found our accountability partner, we have weighed the pros and cons of changing our ways, and we are fully committed to the obstacles that will come along this journey. To overcome obstacles, we have explored the importance of isolation and being okay with that loneliness. During that loneliness one of the main things we should focus on is preparation. This is where the real work happens. During this phase of change it is imperative that we use self- liberation and refrain from dependencies on social liberation.

Self-liberation involves allowing ourselves to be free from societal ideas and pressure. This freedom will come from within. It will be our positive thoughts of affirmation and self-love that will overpower any doubts. Our intent to change the generational cycle should stay in the forefront of our mind. We are sacrificing money to pay off debt because we want to! We are asking family to pitch in with childcare because we need to save more. It is imperative that we feed our soul with the fuel needed to make a plan that is both manageable and realistic.

Stay far from the social liberation we talked about last chapter. Every friend will not understand and that is okay! Just show them we mean business and they just may fall suite. If not, that is okay too. We should not force our life choices onto others. As we evolve, we will lose some folks along the way.

To build wealth it is imperative that we are debt free and that we are maintaining a good credit score. Being free from the monthly car payments, mortgage payments, credit card bills and student loans will free up a large chunk of income. This alleviation from recurring payments will give us the capital to save and sow into investments. These investments will then produce ROI for us to begin wealth building.

As we prepare for our debt free journey, this preparation stage should involve us defining our credit restoration plan and developing a realistic budget.

A credit score is a three-digit number that is used to tell lenders how worthy we are of borrowing and what interest we should pay on borrowing. When we apply for debt, lenders need a reliable way of determining if they should lend to us. Often, they will look to the FICO Score. The Fair Isaac Corporation (FICO) provides the FICO score as an industry standard that is fair to lenders and nondiscriminatory to borrows. This score is calculated using five main factors.

The largest portion of the credit score (35%) comes from us making on time bill payments. Not every lender chooses to report with the credit bureau though. For example, most rental companies do not report the rent we pay on the 1st of each month. We can always ask them to begin reporting on-time payments though. This is an easy way to increase our score and get recognition for the bills we are paying on time. We must be fearless in our self-advocacy. Knock down every door if needed. We must be vocal about the change we wish to see.

The second largest factor of our FICO score (30%) is the amount of debt we owe. This component weighs the amount of debt we owe, in comparison to how much credit left available to us. It is recommended that at any point in time, we have at least 70% of total credit available to spend. For example, we have a $1,000 credit card. Every month, it is priority that we have at least $700 available to spend and a max of $300 in debt that we owe.

This is where we can really get lost financially because households with the lowest net worth hold the highest amount of credit card debt - an average of $10,308 in credit card debt to be exact. When we do not have a rainy-day fund, we find ourselves stuck with the only option to take out debt. This debt looks like pay day loans, personal loans, opening a new credit card or maxing out existing credit cards. According to LendingTree research, those identified as white have about "$7,942 in debt – the highest amount of any racial group. Asians have an average credit card debt of $7,660. Black householders carried the least debt, with an average of $6,172, is 20% lower than the nationwide mean."

With the systemic oppression in the black community, we would think that having a low amount of debt is a good sign of progress. However, it depends on how we look at this. Black households carry less debt because we are least likely to be awarded credit in the first place. Poverty, discrimination, low credit scores, and a lack of access to banking are just a few reasons that we are denied entry to traditional credit options. This leaves us wedded to pay day loans and other lending options with higher interest rates and smaller repayment periods.

The third largest component of our FICO score calculation is based on the length of time we have had access to credit. 15% of this three-digit score looks at the length of time of our oldest and new newest accounts. Additionally, it focuses on the last time we have had to use these accounts. I caution you that, it is possible to have new lines of credit and still have a great score. If we are making on time payments, keeping a low outstanding balance and the accounts are all new it is possible to have a good credit score.

The last two components of our FICO score, accounting for 10% each factor, are the mix of credit and inquiries. The mix of credit refers to the different types of credit we have available to us. For example, owing money on a mortgage in good standing, having debt owed on student loans that are not delinquent, paying on a small business loan, and making monthly credit card payments is a mix of different types of credit.

Inquiries are very tricky to manage, and I find that it is the area that we know the least about! Although they only account for 10% of our credit score, they can knock our score down a few points. To understand, we should differentiate between hard and soft inquiries.

Hard inquiries happen when we apply for credit, and the lender needs to request a copy of our report. Even if we decide not to receive lending from the institution, having our credit report pulled is a hard inquiry. Too many hard inquires in a short period of time appears that we are financially unstable and scrambling for resources. Also, opening too many accounts in a shorter period shortens the length of credit and we have learned that this accounts for 15% of our FICO score. Hard inquires stay on our credit report for 2 years.

A soft inquiry happens when we check our own score and when we seek "pre-approval" for credit. Soft inquires do not impact our score since they are not tied to an actual application for credit. I recommend only applying for credit when we absolutely must. I also advise that we do as much research as we can regarding the lender prior to applying for credit. It is useful to check your score regularly to ensure that hard inquires stem from credit that you applied for and not a result of fraud.

The Credit Restoration Cycle

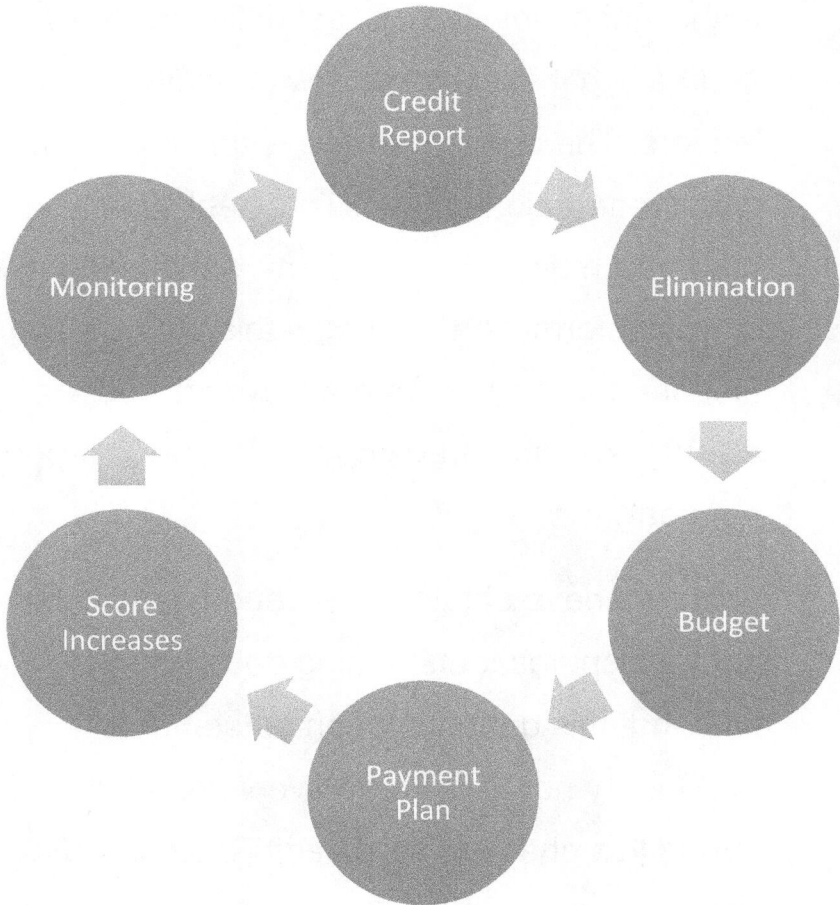

Maintaining good credit is a key ingredient to building wealth. Without it, we find ourselves in this unhealthy cycle of establishing wealth and having it sucked away with debt owed to lenders. The diagram above is taken from my credit restoration course. To establish or reestablish good credit it starts with having current information. To begin this process, we first need a copy of our credit report. We are all entitled to one free copy of our credit report per year.

Once we have obtained the report, we should notate disputes, outstanding debt, and the time that this debt has been outstanding (DOT). Try not to become overwhelmed during this phase of the Credit Restoration Cycle. On the surface, it will seem unmanageable and terribly hard to tackle. However, we will approach this credit report using the new gems that we have learned about obstacles. Boss up! We are capable! Now that we have made a list of items that may be fraudulent, the debt that we owe, and the date that this debt was reported on your credit report we can move on to the second phase of the cycle.

Negative information such as late payments, debt sent to collection agencies and accounts that have not been paid in full will fall off our credit report after 7 years. Although we may have this massive list of debt we owe, we will work to eliminate some of this! To aid in this elimination process we should use the list we developed in phase 1. On our list of debt, cross out any outstanding debt that has been on the credit report for 5 or more years. This debt has been around for some time and it would be wise to focus on newer dings to our credit. We will allow this debt to fall off within the next few years and shift our focus to newer debt.

For the outstanding debt remaining, notate the interest percentage being applied. From here, we have three main options to pay off debt.

Our first option is to pay off our debt by first tackling the liability with the highest interest percentage. Choosing to first pay off obligations with high interest rates saves more money in the long run.

The second option we have is to pay off debt with the lower balances first. I recommend this method for those of us that are new to using self-discipline to navigate our finances. This method is also great for those who have tried to increase their score in the past but may have gotten off course. When we first pay off debt with smaller obligations, we get the instant gratification and the reward of checking a debt obligation from the list. This obviously boosts our self-esteem. This achievement will also improve our outlook on the ability we have to build generational wealth.

The third option is to resolve debt by the type. It would be a great idea to eliminate the car loan soon being that the asset quickly depreciates. With this option, try paying off the car note while the mileage is still low. If we want to sell it, we will receive a higher payment for a car with low mileage. Home mortgages and student loans usually carry low interest rates and higher balances. I suggest paying off these debts once we resolve all others.

After we have committed to our plan of attack, we are one step closer to developing a great credit score, saving money and building generational wealth.

We are now in the budgeting phase of the Credit Restoration Cycle. In this phase we should make a detailed list of our IBM (Income, Bills and Miscellaneous Expenses). This list should be as detailed and accurate as possible.

Do not lie to yourself and be realistic! Lying is only a set up for long term disappointment. If we underestimate our budget now, we will always appear to be overbudget. We did not overspend. Our budget was just off to begin with.

Like most goals, budgets are best accomplished in small manageable chunks. Do not try to be overaggressive with a 5-year budget. Start with budgeting for the next 3 months to 1 year. Yes, saving for retirement and other long-term goals is a key component to wealth building. However, we do not want to overwhelm ourselves. We will also have more money to allocate to long term goals when we get rid of petty debt such as credit cards, personal loans and car payments.

Income

For those of us that are new to wealth building, the income section of our budget is the easiest to approach. We are simply calculating the amount of money we make per month. This will probably consist of earnings from our full-time job, child support, alimony and any government subsidies we receive. We should start with listing all the income we receive monthly. As we progress into our journey to wealth building, we eventually learn to diversify our income. Soon we begin to see income from interest, small business income, investments and more!

Bills

Bills, bills, bills! This is the section of our budget that will be relatively fixed from month to month. In the short term, we will have these same bills every month with seasonal spikes in certain items such as utilities. However, in the long term this is debt we are looking to decrease. These are our credit card payments, mortgages, car payments, and education loans. Being able to timely pay our "bills" each month counts for 35% of our FICO score calculation. This section of our budget is usually the cause of our everyday stress.

The pressure to provide shelter and other basic living necessities becomes the root of physical, mental, spiritual and emotional stress. Research shows that ongoing financial stress leads to heart disease, headaches, and sleep problems. With less disposable money, of course we are unable to seek medical treatment. Now we are forced to take on another bill – the cost of prescriptions. We have learned that unhealthy coping mechanisms leave us SOLID. On a day to day, this looks like, buying more unhealthy foods, taking frequent trips to the mall and avoiding home because we are afraid to be alone. Practicing these unhealthy habits leads to us to drowning our money in miscellaneous expenses.

Miscellaneous Expenses

The last component of our budget is Miscellaneous expenses. Our ability to manage this portion of our budget is a direct reflection of how we manage our stress, our pain and our joy. In short, it is a direct reflection of how we handle change.

To make different the form, nature, context, and/or future course is to change. We are so attached to who we are and how we have existed to this point. Having that older version of us become unrecognizable can be freaking scary! Too afraid of self-discipline and FOMO, we mask the change with unhealthy habits.

Miscellaneous expenses are the catch all category of the budget. This section can include monthly, periodic or yearly expenses. These are everyday extras that support our lifestyle. This is where most families spend most of their income. Rarely do we even remember what we spent it on! Unfortunately, we look up to realize that we have bled through our miscellaneous budget and now we are dipping into our savings!

You are not alone.

To start our miscellaneous expenses budget, start with looking at the calendar. Write in all the birthdays that usually involve spending money! Even if it is just a birthday card for grandpa. Since we are making our budget for the next 3 to 6 months, assign a budget for each birthday. We know the friends that like to live it up and we know the friends that will be appreciative of a gift card to their favorite store. Make your budget for each birthday realistic to the person and to what is happening at the time. If their birthday is during holiday season, and you know that they want to take a trip, it would be a good idea to begin saving for that trip now.

Using this same calendar, begin writing in time frames that you get oil changes and other maintenance done to your car. Maybe, it is routine to get maintenance handled in the fall right before winter weather approaches. Also, in line with car maintenance, include the date to renew our car registration. For this item, I like to budget on the higher end. In the state of California, we cannot renew our registration without paying off outstanding tickets. I usually have let at least two unpaid tickets slip through the cracks. With interest, these tickets are about an extra $300 added to the cost of renewing my vehicle registration. Paying for car insurance premiums for the full policy period is a good cost savings tip. Fronting the bill in advance is always cheaper than making monthly car insurance payments. If we can afford this, make sure that the payment dates are included in the calendar. Since this is not a monthly bill, we may forget when the time comes to pay for our upcoming policy period. On the other hand, if we are making monthly payments, this expense qualifies as a Bill rather a Miscellaneous expense.

Next, write in when you expect to go shopping for new clothing. Personally, I like to shop at the end of each season for the next and maybe one shopping trip in the middle of each season. Again, this is the part where honesty comes into play. Right now, do not focus on our ambition to change. The goal is to document where we currently are in life.

I do not have any children yet but be sure that you include your family and pets in your personal budget! Each relationship handles finances differently! Over the last 10 years, I have learned so much about managing finances as a couple. I can go on and on about the dynamics at play. Stay tuned for future books dedicated to navigating money in a relationship. In this literature we are focusing on YOU and YOUR conscious decision to live the life you want to live.

If you and your spouse are splitting the cost for your kid's miscellaneous expenses, be sure to include these numbers. The little ones are constantly growing so scheduling their shopping trips would be extremely helpful! Do not leave out the extra-curricular activities, summer camps, and back to school supplies. For our fur babies, the calendar should include grooming and veterinary appointments. Also, for our fur babies, we should make sure we include the monthly cost of their food with our Bills.

Health is wealth! In this climate we have learned the importance of self-care. The COVID-19 pandemic and the movement for social justice has provoked a heaviness to hover over all of us. It is imperative that we continue to maintain our peace and Zen. The miscellaneous budget should include the vacations, candles, organization dues, vitamins, doctor's visits, exercise supplies and all the things that help support our peace.

Lastly, let us not forget about seasonal expenses! Start with making a list of people we would like to buy Christmas gifts for and assign a budget for each person. Begin the communication around whose hosting Thanksgiving, Christmas and Easter dinner. These things may seem small, but hosting is a big responsibility! We usually will buy new décor for our home, hire landscaping help, and spare no expenses on the menu. Do not forget about relationship anniversaries! Commonly, our anniversaries include a gift swap or a vacation. Communication is key, so get these conversations started now during this planning period.

Using the diagram below, calculate your disposable income. To do this, add up your income, subtract your bills and subtract your miscellaneous expenses.

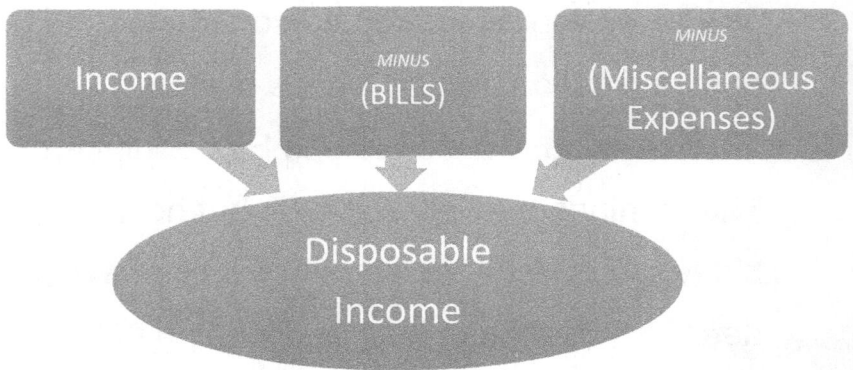

Now that we have calculated our Disposable Income, we are ready to move on to making our payment plan. We are one step closer to building good credit. Hang in there!

The payment plan phase of the Credit Restoration Cycle involves us taking a deep dive into PASS. This is an acronym that includes the four ingredients needed to develop a solid payment plan. We should develop a Payment timeline, define the Amount we are comfortable with paying per month, call creditors to see if Settling debt is an option, and Set up Auto Pay.

Settling Debts

Debt settlement is a way to resolve an outstanding balance without paying the full amount. The lender provides us with a lump sum payment that can reduce 10% to 50% of our debt. How much we are offered depends a lot on how much we owe. The goal is to save money by paying less interest. We have the option to hire a debt settlement firm to represent us or to settle debt directly with the lender ourselves. I recommend the latter. Take out the middleman and represent yourself.

To settle your debt always know how much you are willing to pay of the total amount. Be prepared to negotiate their counteroffer. Although it is a lump sum payment, we can speak with the lender about securing a payment today and paying the rest over our next few paychecks. Most lenders will allow us to settle. However, I have found it a bit difficult to settle with medical bills.

Payment Timeline and Amount

Remember, we have the option to pay off debt in order of highest to lowest interest rate, the type of debt we have, or the amount of outstanding debt in order of smallest to largest amount.

The payment timeline and the monthly amount will be defined for us If decide to work through debt settlement. If not, we must define how many months we want to dedicate our money to paying off each obligation.

Making monthly payments equal to the minimum amount due is not going to cut it! Due to interests, it costs us more in the long run if we are just making just the minimum payment. With the compounding of interest, our outstanding balance will continue to rise and cause our credit score to drop. Remember, that 30% of our FICO credit score relates to the credit utilization ratio. This is how much we owe to the lender, divided by our credit limit.

Start with looking at the budget we developed in the last phase of the Credit Restoration Cycle. Our disposable income will be the starting figure to develop our payment timeline and monthly payment amount. Take the debt that you want to tackle first and divide it by a timeline that you are comfortable with. As an example, we are paying off our car note of $13,000 and our disposable income is $1,500. I would suggest taking this $13,000 and dividing it by 12 months. Doing so would equal a monthly payment of $1,083.33.

This is a comfortable payment to make with our disposable income because we still have $400 remaining to save each month. We are not super concerned with saving in this phase of wealth building. Getting out of debt is the focus! This extra $400 a month will accumulate an emergency fund for us. Once we are free from the excess bills, we will be able to increase savings and diversify investments.

Set up Auto-Pay

Auto pay has been the leading factor to my on-time payment history. Urges will come and we may fall victim to excess miscellaneous spending. In all that fun, we should still make sure our bills are paid in full and on time. Trying to keep an eye on our bill calendar leaves room for error. Taking the manual effort out of paying bills has led to a reduction in interest and in late fees.

Action

The Transtheoretical Model found that change only happens when we want it to. They also found that healthy behaviors can only be adapted through a cycle of intentional change. The time we spend moving through the phases is variable, but the action steps needed to make true progress are not. Take your time in each phase of this cycle. Recognize that we are morphing in to this stronger, healthier version of us. This process will take time, discipline, and courage.

The thing with change, is that it is observable! Since we must see it, there is action required to produce the change. We can excel at precontemplation, contemplation and planning. However, without action we are merely brainstorming. The only person that needs to observe this change is you. It is dangerous to become fixated with receiving affirmation from our friends and family. This is not their journey! We believe in our ability to build long term wealth and we know that we are doing the work to get there. However, our friends may not share the same optimistic view. This does not mean that they love us less. I have found that people will transfer their limitations and self-doubt right on to us! Since they have not been able to achieve it, they may not even believe that our goals are feasible! Helping relationships, stimulus control and self-liberation are three techniques that can help to keep our thoughts and actions in parallel.

Trying to change bad behaviors that society normalizes can cause extreme loneliness. We will not be able to make every brunch, game night and event that our friends organize. We are now the friend that will not come out, even when invited. Maybe we can only come out here and there! Remember to stick to only the events on our budget calendar! Our friends will either adapt and give us advance notice, or they deal with our absence. This is not forever! This abstinence only occurs while we are in this phase of resolving debt and the months thereafter that we begin to build our savings. Our accountability partner will be our mentor and best friend! Be open, be honest, and be vulnerable with them. At this point, they are the only person that truly knows our commitment.

For this relationship to work out, there must be some ground rules in place. Rule 1 is to define what we want from your accountability partner. We should clearly communicate what we need from them and the system of communication. The schedule can become monthly, biweekly, quarterly or whatever works for the pair. Having a set time to catch up will make those low moments seem a little less grey. We are not going to feel completely confident every day. It is helpful to know that although we are in a bad space currently, tomorrow or next week we get to check in with someone who understands. The final rule to effectively using our accountability partner is to simply value them! This relationship should be a priority of ours. What we get out of the mentorship will be equivalent to the energy we put into it.

Stimulus control occurs when we re-engineer the environment to have reminders and signs that support our healthy behaviors. If a person only shops excessively when with friends, then the social environment is the stimulus that drives the over shopping. Those experienced at wealth building realize that we must remain under "stimulus control" of our environments. We must stay on cruise control, with our UV shades on, blocking out every possible distraction. Issues usually come about when we get sucked into short term indulgences like Instagram, rather than long term tasks such as creating our budget. The environment will always throw us a curve ball, but it is our duty to control the stimuli and stay in the driver's seat of our finances.

We have talked about self-liberation earlier in the preparation phase of the TTM. This process to maintain change requires an ongoing effort to affirm our beliefs. We should not rely on others to justify the means to our end. Try writing down a few affirmations that you want to remember each day. It would be helpful to recite these declarations as many times as necessary. I recommend that these affirmations are also shared with accountability partners. Remember that they are an important part of this journey and that they can only hold us accountable to the goals we share.

At this point in our wealth building journey, we have evaluated our credit report, created a budget, prepared a payment plan, and began to make timely monthly payments. Using PASS, we are now on the track to credit recovery. Now that we are in action mode, we must learn how to deal with increases to our credit score and learn how to monitor our progress.

Our credit score will increase as the risk of lending to us decreases. We are now on the road to creating a better track record. This gratification will boost our self-esteem and our commitment to wealth building. However, this joy can have us running back to those old coping mechanisms. When we see our score tick, it is easy to think that the battle is won.

There are a few techniques we should keep in our practice when we notice increases to our credit.

Do not take on new debt while in the process of paying off existing debt. Lenders are made aware of positive changes to our credit score. As a result, we begin to receive pre-approval notices for debt options, and it can be very tempting. There are a few reasons not to accept these offers. Inquiries contribute to the calculation of our FICO score. Taking on new debt requires the lender to run a hard credit inquiry. Remember, that every hard inquiry can cause our credit score to drop by a few points. In addition, we have not completely paid off all our debt. Making the decision to apply for new credit early in the process completely defeats the point! Our score is not yet at its peak!

Another factor to maintaining good credit, is the mix of credit types that we have. Deciding to rip open another credit card or taking on another car note is not the best idea right now! Instead, we need to save our money to purchase our next car in cash! The goal is not to pay off debt to take on new debt eventually. We instead want to pay off our debt and live a life of less stress.

With new achievements come a greater increase in responsibility. People are always watching. We are still growing and evolving and perhaps not at the greatest point to help others. It is wise to avoid co-signing on loans for friends and family. Although we are in isolation, our circle is aware of our journey to wealth building. We never know the affect our actions can have on others. During this time, people may feel comfortable confiding in us with their financial issues. Both us, and our credit score are in a fragile state. One false move can be a major set-back. Co-signing on loans are always a risk. We have no clue if the other signer will make timely payments. If they default on the loan, that debt becomes ours. This new debt of course affects our credit utilization rate, our payment timeline, and our overall confidence. Again, the goal is to pay off our debt and to stay debt free.

Lastly, in this phase do not close out any existing accounts you have. Closing out existing accounts increases your credit utilization rate because you have less of a balance available to you. In addition, having older accounts on your credit report shows lenders that you have maintained great standing over a longer duration of time.

During this time, we should be making our pre-arranged payments, saving our disposable income, and researching future investment opportunities. Although we do not have the cash currently, I want to stress the importance of taking this time to define the life we want to live in the future. Refer to the goals that we created earlier. We should be thinking of how we will increase our sources of income after our debt is paid off. Think about how we felt only having bi-weekly income to add to the budget. If stocks are of interests, take these months or years to simply watch the market. When ready, dip your toe in with minimal cash output. I recommend that this action phase be full of new information and new ideas. It is recommended that we find friends that are in our areas of interest. The people we choose to surround ourselves with can be the pathway to opportunity.

During the Credit Restoration Cycle, the final pit stop is monitoring. This phase is less complex than the others. After putting in all that work to increase our credit score it only makes sense that we do the work to maintain this score long term. To monitor credit, I would suggest finding a credit monitoring program. These days a lot of the larger banking institutions offer free credit monitoring to their customers. We should complete this research in month one of our payment plan. The first month that we make a lump sum payment to our credit will be followed by score increases. We will only know of these increases with the help of a monitoring program.

Identity theft is one of the fastest growing online crimes. Now that we have good credit we are certainly more at risk. According to Forbes, the victims that are most at risk are those that have opened new credit within the last 6 months. Credit monitoring software will alert you immediately about fraudulent activity.

GAS

GROWING AND SOWING

GAS, this chapter of the book, is the final stop along this journey together. According to Oxford Languages, a gas is a substance or matter in a state in which it expands freely. In this state, the gas grows to fill the whole of a container, having no fixed shape (unlike a solid) and no fixed volume (unlike a liquid). Our acronym for GAS, is **GROWING AND SOWING**. We are growing into the CEO of our lives and sowing the seeds to build long term wealth.

Maintenance

We must keep our foot on the gas! The contemplation, planning and immediate action is behind us. Maintenance is the everyday action to ensure that our growth is in line with the life we want to live.

To work on our individual growth, my boyfriend and I took a year away from our relationship. Having spent years together since the age of 17, we decided to do some adulting alone for a while. This decision did not happen overnight, but the change to my pockets sure did! Going from splitting expenses to paying every bill on my own was a huge reality check. I was grateful for this newfound freedom but there were some serious life changes that I needed to make. Prior to the split I had paid off all my credit card debt, I resolved medical bills and I had gotten my credit score to a great point. All my disposable income was obviously going towards paying off debt. This did not leave much cash to save. At the time, I had only saved up about $2,500. This money was not going to be enough to pay the security deposit for my new apartment, the last month's rent at my old apartment with him, and the cost of moving. Did I mention furniture? Unfortunately, I had to take out a personal loan to afford these expenses and stay current with bills and miscellaneous expenses. I was extremely grateful that I could get approved for a personal loan with a low interest rate. There was a time in life where lenders would not allow me to borrow at all! I could not believe that I had relapsed. I paid all my debt but here I was taking out a personal loan. I thought that I was growing and sowing! Things will happen in life, and all we can control is our response to the change.

When life throws you lemons, you make lemonade! I enjoyed this year of life. It gave me the opportunity to meet new people and to focus on my personal growth. I quickly paid off the loan without missing one payment. I developed this mindset that I was "broke," and I lived on a tight budget. I was infamous for saying that I did not have the money and I lived shamelessly in that reality. Did I have the money? Absolutely! However, I only had the money for saving. I did not want to become consumed with the freedom of my new lifestyle. The cost of going out with the girls adds up! Living alone allowed me to just eat whatever I found in the cabinet for dinner. This was a huge contrast to the responsibility of cooking for two.

As secretive as I am with my relationship, this story shares the realities of relapse. We usually hear this word associated with drug and alcohol use, but it can relate to other areas of life where we experience a decline in progress. When we experience trials and tribulations it is easy to forget about our wealth building journey. Our natural response is to fight or flight. We must make an intentional decision to fight. How we choose to fight makes all the difference though. Our natural reaction is to overeat, to engage in retail therapy, to ignore the issue, or to cope with drugs. I am going to share with you three key methods to maintain wealth despite life's hurdles.

The first method to maintaining wealth, is to develop healthy keystone habits. Charles Duhigg's book, The Power of Habit, tells us that keystone habits are "small changes or habits that people introduce into their routines that unintentionally carry over into other aspects of their lives." These healthy habits are a direct link to mental clarity. I cannot emphasize how important it is that we approach each day clear headed and full of positive energy. This transparency will provide us with the mental space to create ideas that we can monetize. This clearness will also give us the momentum to work through the struggles of our side business or investments. Keystone habits that we are most familiar with are exercise, prayer, reading, and writing. It is proven that an increase in exercise leads to better sleep, stress reduction, and better eating habits.

Our lifestyle is the second key to maintaining wealth. We do not have to "look rich." Coming from a low-income family, I understand the fascination with buying things to change the public perception. We must get a grip on our need for external affirmation. This external confirmation that we are rich creates a multitude of issues. For one, it attracts the wrong type of company. We spoke earlier about finding like-minded people that support our goals. Second, it creates a mountain of stress. We become consumed with having to look the part around our friends and for the web so much that we lose sight of why we even started our wealth building journey. Before we know it, we are consuming things to keep up with our friendship circle. Lastly, the more we spend on our image the less money we have available to save. Living within on our means is a truth regardless of how much we earn. Experts advice that we spend no more than 30% of our income on housing. Extra earnings do not equate to a nicer car, a larger house, and more clothes. Instead, consider pouring extra earnings into a second home that can be used as a rental property. This extra money can also be used to buy stocks, commercial real estate, gold or startup costs for a business. These are just a few ways to multiply our earnings to create long term wealth.

Time-Management is our final key to maintaining wealth. Managing our money is similar to managing our time. We should create a realistic schedule the same way that we created a realistic budget. Our budget is limited just like the hours in a day. It is important that we map out this time exerting less energy to the activities that do not create long term financial gain. Take watching TV for example. I love to binge Netflix as much as the next person, but to get this book done I had to limit my daily intake. Do not shy away from writing it down! I have invested in quite a few white boards over the years. Writing helps to build memory and if our schedule changes simply adjust!

I want to let you in on a little secret. Owning a home, having good credit, or earning a six-figure salary does not equal wealth. These are simply ingredients that put us on the pathway to begin building wealth. This term wealth is like the term love or happiness. They are all subjective and can mean whatever we define them to be. For some, being able to afford a housekeeper is wealth. While other people may feel that having a chef means that they are wealthy. When we research this term, it simply means to have "an abundance of valuable possessions or money." I like to look at wealth in economic terms. This view tells us to basically total up all our assets and subtract our debts. For the assets this is our home, investments, cash in the bank, patents we may own, and the list continues. Keep in mind that it is possible for this number to be negative. The wealth building goal is to accumulate valuable assets and minimize our debts to the extent we can maintain the lifestyle of our choosing while passing down the remaining wealth to our children.

We can all live a life of *Less Debt, Less Stress.* The amount of money we make is a non-factor. It is about how we spend the money we have. We should not use our socioeconomic status to justify drowning in debt. This financial stress takes hold of our relationships, our lifestyle, and our faith.

It is easy to become content with what we know and who we are. Self-love is the best love. However, self-love involves self-improvement. We all possess unhealthy habits. What separates us is our commitment to taking action on these habits. This action involves us budgeting, staying committed to our plan of attack and saving. During this time, we are focused on research for future investments and our dedication to building wealth.

The life we want to live has never been clearer. It is up to us to do the work to make this dream a reality. We have the Transtheoretical Model to guide our cognitive behavior and the Credit Restoration Cycle to guide our every-day habits. We are now ready to live a life of Less Debt, Less Stress.

www.ingramcontent.com/pod-product-compliance
Lightning Source LLC
Chambersburg PA
CBHW060356050426
42449CB00009B/1758